ideals®
FRIENDSHIP

More Than 50 Years of Celebrating Life's Most Treasured Moments

Vol. 57, No. 4

You meet your friend, your face brightens—
you have struck gold.—*Rassia*

IDEALS—Vol. 57, No. 4 July MM IDEALS (ISSN 0019-137X)
is published six times a year: January, March, May, July, September, and November by
IDEALS PUBLICATIONS INCORPORATED,
535 Metroplex Drive, Suite 250, Nashville, TN 37211.
Periodical postage paid at Nashville, Tennessee, and additional mailing offices.
Copyright © MM by IDEALS PUBLICATIONS INCORPORATED.
POSTMASTER: Send address changes to Ideals, PO Box 305300,
Nashville, TN 37230. All rights reserved.

Title IDEALS registered U.S. Patent Office.
SINGLE ISSUE—U.S. $5.95 USD; Higher in Canada
ONE-YEAR SUBSCRIPTION—U.S. $19.95 USD; Canada $36.00 CDN (incl. GST and shipping); Foreign $25.95 USD
TWO-YEAR SUBSCRIPTION—U.S. $35.95 USD; Canada $66.50 CDN (incl. GST and shipping); Foreign $47.95 USD

Subscribers may call customer service at 1-800-558-4343 to make address changes.
Unsolicited manuscripts will not be returned without a self-addressed, stamped envelope.

ISBN 0-8249-1162-8   GST 131903775

Visit *Ideals*'s website at www.idealspublications.com

Cover
FLOWERS FOR A FRIEND
Mark Scott, Photographer
FPG International

Inside Front Cover
BOWL OF NASTURTIUMS
Felix Vallotton, Artist
Christie's Images

Inside Back Cover
SPELLBOUND
Charles Moreau, Artist
Fine Art Photographic Library
Ltd./Private Collection

Song of Summer

Edna Jackson Burrows

I sing of mellow nights and sun-drenched skies;
Of bees with nectar darting in and out
Among the tinted petals; butterflies
In showy colors flitting roundabout.
As spring slips gently by, the yellow grain
Is reaped and stacked to dry beneath the sun;
The ripening odors sweep the hill and plain
Before the harvest days are well begun.
What sweets are sealed in autumn fruits again,
For sunny beams have touched each tree and plant.
What painted blossoms grow in wood and glen
With honeyed perfumes ready to enchant.
I trim the garden in a secret way,
A fairyland of blooms for each bouquet.

When We But Dream

Sarah Bridge Graves

Just mention summer and the days become
A cloudy blueness, shadowy and sweet.
And every single person that you greet
Remarks how fine the weather; how bees hum
Inside a Canterbury bell and dust
Themselves with golden pollen, bearing
Its richness to adjoining flowers, sharing
Their dinner music with each hungry thrust;
That dogs sleep in the patchwork shade of trees
And cats recline upon petunia beds
Seems foreordained within their furry heads,
Just as birds fly aloft when there's a breeze.
Life falls into a pattern old and dear
When we but dream of summertime each year.

A bed of hollyhocks and a thriving vine soften a colonial facade at the St. Gaudens National Monument in Cornish, New Hampshire. Photo by Johnson's Photography.

BY AN
INLAND LAKE

William Stanley Braithwaite

Long drawn, the cool, green shadows
Steal o'er the lake's warm breast,
And the ancient silence follows
The burning sun to rest.
The calm of a thousand summers
And dreams of countless Junes
Return when the lake wind murmurs
Thro' golden August noons.

AUGUST

Celia Thaxter

Buttercup nodded and said good-bye;
Clover and daisy went off together,
But the fragrant water lilies lie
Yet moored in the golden August weather.
The swallows chatter about their flight;
The cricket chirps like a rare good fellow;
The asters twinkle in clusters bright
While the corn grows ripe and the
    apples mellow.

Left: Pink and white water lilies float atop Ames Pond in Stonington, Maine. Photo by Johnson's Photography.
Overleaf: A border garden in Manitowoc, Wisconsin, is crowned by a profusion of lilies. Photo by Darryl R. Beers.

BITS & PIECES

Swing, swing,
Sing, sing,
Here's my throne, and I am a king!
Swing, sing,
Swing, sing,
Farewell earth, for I'm on the wing!

—*William Allingham*

Sweet childish days that were as
long as twenty days are now.

—*William Wordsworth*

Ignore dull days; forget the showers;
Keep count of only shining hours.

—*from the German,*
adapted by
Louis Untermeyer

Jolly boating weather
And a hay harvest breeze,
Blade on the feather,
Shade off the trees,
Swing, swing together
With your body between your knees.

—*William Cory*

*S*ummer afternoon—summer
afternoon; to me those have always
been the two most beautiful words
in the English language.
                    —*Henry James*

*S*ummer's lease hath
all too short a date.
          —*William Shakespeare*

*T*he wood . . . is now with
glorious colors blest.
O children, haste
To enjoy its treat,
And where gay flowers grow,
swing your feet.
                    —*Nithart*

*H*ow do you like to go up in a swing,
Up in the air so blue?
Oh, I do think it the pleasantest thing
Ever a child can do!
          —*Robert Louis Stevenson*

EVERY CHILD WAS KING . . . IN A SWING

Marjorie Holmes

Today, many a child who has a yard to play in also is the casual possessor of his own "playground set." This is a very efficient and ingenious combination of poles and chains upon which are arranged excellent if somewhat smaller editions of much of the equipment to be found on regulation playgrounds—swings, seesaws, rings, trapezes, and often a slide.

When I was a child in Storm Lake, to have such marvels on your own doorstep would be like having rubbed Aladdin's lamp. Such equipment as we had with which to vent our boundless energies we mostly contrived out of rope, old boards, and imagination. Or for the really polished pleasure we took a leisurely jaunt to the park.

There was in this park a magnificent array of clanking, shining playground equipment. The chain swings were both perilous and popular. They too seemed to us gallow-tall. If you were a good pumper, or had a good strong pumping partner, there would be a sudden thrilling buckle and jerk as you soared skyward. This everybody interpreted as warning that you were on the very verge of "going over." To actually "go over" the top bar was rumored to be a thrilling, appalling, and heroic disaster. Kids were always claiming they had "gone over," but we knew better, if only because they survived unmaimed. I never knew personally anyone who had met this mysterious and grimly enticing fate, but the legends abounded.

Also, once firmly ensconced in a swing, a child was king. Nothing short of an earthquake (or a parental summons) could force him to abdicate if he didn't want to. When we encountered one of these stubborn characters the best we could do was hurl taunts from the more humble nearby teeter-totters, proving our scorn for the compromise by the fury with which we banged and bounced them, or walked their slanting boards.

You didn't really have to go to the park, however—not if you had a good imagination and a big yard. . . . The genuine, most permanent attraction of every yard worthy of the name was the swing. Even childless homes usually had a swing of some kind. The status symbol of the era, particularly for elderly, genteel people, was a wooden affair with two seats face-to-face which glided back and forth on a little slatted platform. To visit a home so richly endowed was bliss. The children made a beeline for the contraption, fought over turns to be conductor, and transformed it instantly into a streetcar or a train.

For steady, day-to-day comfort and pleasure, though, the best swing of all was the old-fashioned rope kind in your own backyard. It occupied a unique and special place in the life of a child—half person, half thing. A swing could be shared—pushing or being pushed, or pumping. But a swing could be used alone. A swing was like a faithful friend waiting for you when there was nobody else to play with: You could wind up in it and feel the world spin, lean over its seat on your tummy and watch the lazily gliding ground, climb onto it and, grasping its hairy hands with your own, propel yourself into a leafy, dancing space.

You were king in a swing; it was your royal chariot, your soaring throne. The ropes creaked and sighed companionably to your swooping, and the joints of the old maple tree joined the secret conversation.

It was unthinkable not to have such a swing. And when the old one wore out, or was about to, your father brought a thick yellow coil of new rope home from the hardware store and set about replacing it. Or your grandpa did. Our Grandpa Griffith prided himself on making the seat. Curly shavings piled up as he lovingly whittled and planed and carved and with his big, bonehandled jack-knife notched the middle.

A young boy and girl of yesteryear enjoy the thrills of a swing. Photos from Superstock.

Then while an admiring audience gathered, Dad would shinny up the tree, bits of bark raining down. He would scramble out onto the limb to test its strength. Thump, the old rope would fall in a serpentine twining, and we would snatch it up and prance about with it.

Catching the new one from below, Dad would make lovely golden loops, baring and gritting his teeth as he knotted them securely, in a way that we always associated with intense endeavor on his part. We all thought him remarkably brave and strong, and watched his maneuvers as awed as if he were a mountain climber. The climax would come when he sailed out on the rope and dangled for a minute, then slid down it fireman-style.

The children rushed to claim the swing, fighting for turns, pumping singly or by twos. A new swing always seemed to be filled with such joy and vigor and power; its muscles distended, it squealed and seemed to go higher. (Or were we only always getting older and stronger to make its newness match our will?) A pair of good pumpers could send it whipping into the branches, almost into the stars. And like the chain swings in the park, it too would buckle as if threatening to hurl you over some mysterious pinnacle of fear and delight.

Thank goodness the ancient clanking swings remain—swings tall enough to "go over." For it is these the kids still clamor to use. They stand like monuments to the days when play was intense and wild and wonderful. When every house had a swing. When imagination meant more than money, and any child with a yard, a length of rope, a board, a tree, could be an acrobat, an equestrian, a king!

What Johnny Told Me

John Ciardi

I went to play with Billy.

He

Threw my cap into a tree.

I threw his glasses in the ditch.

He

dipped my shirt

in a bucket of pitch.

I hid his shoes in the garbage can.

And

then we heard

the ice cream man.

So I bought him a cone.

He

bought me one.

A true good friend is a lot of fun!

Artist Donald Zolan depicts the joys of shared ice cream and shared friendship in THE KISS. *Image copyright © Zolan Fine Arts, Ltd., Hershey, Pennsylvania.*

Neighbor's Garden

Sudie Stuart Hager

Her garden captures every eye that passes,
For it's the strangest mixture ever seen—
Tall larkspur, squat petunias, bearded grasses,
An untrimmed hedge, a towering evergreen,
Flame poppies, creamy zinnias, mauve-blue phlox,
Gray ragweeds, purple thistles, long-necked gourds,
Alert, bright pansies, drowsy four-o'clocks,
Thick-crested cockscombs, iris's thin leaf-swords.

"A garden's like the world," is neighbor's claim,
"All kinds of life must grow along together;
Without some weeds, 'twould be too perfect—tame—
Too tender-bred, things cannot stand the weather."

And folks must like her garden just that way,
Because they wander in, relax, and stay.

Well now, and while the summer stays,
Profit by these garden days.
　　　—Robert Louis Stevenson

Late summer color explodes in this Missouri garden. Photo by Gay Bumgarner.

From My Garden Journal

Deana Deck

STRAWFLOWERS

One of the nice things about having a garden is being able to share flowers with friends. Flowers are always welcome, whether as a housewarming gift, a get-well encouragement, or a friendly gesture.

I particularly enjoy sharing "everlasting" flowers, such as strawflowers, that won't wilt in a week. These blossoms dry easily and maintain their colors once dried. I have given fresh bouquets in summer with a card enclosed explaining how to dry them and colorful, dried bouquets in winter as a reminder of warm days past.

Many years ago, when I first began growing and drying strawflowers, I researched garden books to determine the optimal growing conditions—a first step in planting anything. When I looked up strawflowers, I encountered a familiar problem: because I only knew the flower by its common name, numerous species were listed as being strawflowers.

Luckily I had a couple of photo encyclopedias, so I quickly compared the species names from the garden books with the photographs in my encyclopedias. As I looked over the pictures to find the flower I thought was the strawflower, I discovered that strawflowers can vary in appearance, origin, and growth.

Bracteantha Bracteata, also known as everlasting daisy, has large and decorative blossoms ranging in color from yellow to rusty-red with yellow centers. These blossoms usually appear singly on the stem, although some types produce a small cluster of blossoms at the end of a flowering branch. The everlasting daisy is a three-foot-tall annual that performs as a perennial in Zones 8 through 11. It prefers moist, well-drained soil in full sun. Propagated by seed in northern climates or by tip cuttings in the Deep South, the everlasting daisy will bloom from summer to early fall.

The *Helichrysum* species has several types of strawflowers known as paper daisies. One, the silver strawflower, *H. Milfordiae*, is a creeping perennial from the sub-alpine areas of South Africa. Hardy only in Zones 7 through 10, it is not frost tolerant but thrives in mild climates with low summer humidity such as the southern Appalachians. It prefers a warm, sunny position and gritty, well-drained soil that is not too fertile.

Another *Helichrysum* species, *H. Bellidioides*, produces white blossoms and is commonly called the white strawflower. Originally from New Zealand, the white strawflower is a creeper that grows just six inches tall but spreads as much as two feet. Its leaves are tiny, but the blossoms are about an inch and a quarter in diameter and rise above the foliage on long stems. It is also only hardy in Zones 7 through 9 and must be planted and harvested between the spring and fall frosts.

After perusing through these species and sub-species of strawflowers, I finally found the plant I had envisioned when I first began my search: the *Rodanthe*. The pink, yellow, and white flowers of the *Rodanthe* species are particularly prized for drying. Like other strawflowers, this species has to be grown as an annual everywhere in the United States except in Florida and the Gulf states. Native to western Australia, it prefers full sun and well-drained soil of poor quality. In the appropriate zone, this type of strawflower will bloom nearly year round, but for most of the United States it is a summer bloomer only.

The blooms on all species of strawflowers look the same whether fresh or dried. However, their stems are quite weak and will not support the plants when dried. Therefore, the stems need to be supported immediately upon cutting with a thin florist's wire inserted into the blossom. Cut all but about a half inch of the stem, and carefully insert a six- or eight-inch length of twenty-one-gauge florist wire. Be careful not to insert the wire too deeply or it will show at the center of the bloom. Dry the flowers by hanging them upside down in a cool area for three to five weeks. Then, before using the dried strawflowers in an arrangement, wrap the florist wire tightly with florist tape that is slightly elastic, starting at the bloom and working down.

An alternative method to a wrapped wire stem is to use so-called "false stems." These are strong stems from plants such as the poppy, yarrow, delphinium, or goldenrod that have been dried previously. Insert the florist wire into the substitute stem; then place the stump of the strawflower stem directly onto the false stem and glue them together using white craft glue.

The difference between using a wrapped wire stem or a false stem will be apparent. The wire stem can be bent for a more natural look in a bouquet, but the more brittle false stem will only stand upright. Which method you choose will depend on the vase or the arrangement you plan to create.

Each year, I look forward to the end of the summer when I can gather bouquets of strawflowers and hang their colorful blossoms to dry. When giving the dried flowers as housewarming gifts or as tokens of thanks, I often present the arrangement in a pretty vase or basket which becomes a part of the gift. But you will find that strawflowers are just as delightful when they are simply wrapped in colored tissue paper and tied with a ribbon. Unlike a gift of fresh flowers which will be thrown out at the first sign of wilting, a gift of everlasting strawflowers to a friend will serve as a constant reminder of your friendship.

You will find that strawflowers are just as delightful when simply wrapped in colored tissue paper and tied with a ribbon.

Deana Deck tends to her flowers, plants, and vegetables at her home in Nashville, Tennessee, where her popular garden column is a regular feature in The Tennessean.

The Tuft of Flowers

Robert Frost

I went to turn the grass once after one
Who mowed it in the dew before the sun.

The dew was gone that made his blade so keen
Before I came to view the leveled scene.

I looked for him behind an isle of trees;
I listened for his whetstone on the breeze.

But he had gone his way, the grass all mown,
And I must be, as he had been, alone,

'As all must be,' I said within my heart,
'Whether they work together or apart.'

But as I said it, swift there passed me by
On noiseless wing a bewildered butterfly,

Seeking with memories grown dim o'er night
Some resting flower of yesterday's delight.

And once I marked his flight go round and round,
As where some flower lay withering on the ground.

And then he flew as far as eye could see,
And then on tremulous wing came back to me.

I thought of questions that have no reply,
And would have turned to toss the grass to dry;

But he turned first, and led my eye to look
At a tall tuft of flowers beside a brook,

A leaping tongue of bloom the scythe had spared
Beside a reedy brook the scythe had bared.

The mower in the dew had loved them thus,
By leaving them to flourish, not for us,

Nor yet to draw one thought of ours to him,
But from sheer morning gladness at the brim.

The butterfly and I had lit upon,
Nevertheless, a message from the dawn,

That made me hear the wakening birds around,
And hear his long scythe whispering to the ground,

And feel a spirit kindred to my own;
So that henceforth I worked no more alone;

But glad with him, I worked as with his aid,
And weary, sought at noon with him the shade;

And dreaming, as it were, held brotherly speech
With one whose thought I had not hoped to reach.

'Men work together,' I told him from the heart,
'Whether they work together or apart.'

Left: A tuft of asters dots a field of golden grass on New Hampshire's Isles of Shoals. Photo by Johnson's Photography.
Above: A great spangled fritillary butterfly lights upon a coneflower in Missouri. Photo by Gay Bumgarner.

THE TRUE MEASURE

Thelma Anna Martin

Measure time by living—
By the smiles and all the giving,
All the joys that you can heap
Upon a neighbor.

Measure by the dew-laced grasses,
By each wagging tail which passes,
And every joyful piece
Of honest labor.

Measure by each act of sharing,
Every way that speaks of caring,
All the joy-filled interludes
Which give the day its sun.

Measure by each fragrant flower,
Special warmth from every hour;
And you will own true riches
Before the course is run.

A GIFT OF ROSES

Pollyanna Sedziol

There are roses on my desk
That I'd like to share with you;
But roses can't be mailed,
So these words will have to do.

Think of petals touched with sunset,
Gently curled like sleeping hands;
And if you can imagine fragrance,
Blend into it beauty's strands.

In an alabaster vase
Place an infant, early bud,
An opening flower of youth,
And a full-bloomed rose, matured.

Then picture me with pen in hand
Describing them for you,
And you will know how lovingly
You're thought of each day through.

*How I revel in your lovely letters.
Opening one of them is like
plunging into a bath of rose water.*

—William O'Brien to
Sophie Raffalovich, 1890

A rose garden grows up and around a stone barn in Rhode Island's Colt State Park. Photo by Johnson's Photography.

It's a Sweet Thing

Percy Bysshe Shelley

It is a sweet thing, friendship: a dear balm;
A happy and auspicious bird of calm
Which rides o'er life's ever-tumultuous ocean;
A god that broods o'er chaos in commotion;
A flower which, fresh as Lapland roses are,
Lifts its bold head into the world's frore air
And blooms most radiantly when others die—
Health, hope, and youth, and brief prosperity—
And with the light and odor of its bloom,
Shining within the dungeon and the tomb,
Whose coming is as light and music are
Amid dissonance and gloom; a star
Which moves not mid the moving heavens alone;
A smile amid dark frowns; a gentle tone
Among rude voices; a beloved light,
A solitude, a refuge, a delight.

*A wreath of dried flowers, perhaps a gift from a gardening friend, brightens
a garden fence in Galena, Illinois. Photo by Jessie Walker.*

Friendship's Like Music

Francis Quarles

Friendship's like music; two strings tuned alike
Will both stir, though but only one you strike.
It is the quintessence of all perfection
Extracted into one: a sweet connection
Of all the virtues moral and divine,
Abstracted into one. It is a mine,
Whose nature is not rich, unless in making
The state of others wealthy by partaking.
It blooms and blossoms both in sun and shade,
Doth (like a bay in winter) never fade:
It loveth all, and yet suspecteth none;
Is provident, yet seeketh not her own;
'Tis rare itself, yet maketh all things common;
And is judicious, yet judgeth no man.

The perfect model of true friendship's this:
A rare affection of the soul, which is
Begun with ripened judgment; doth persever
With simple wisdom, and concludes with Never.
'Tis pure in substance, as refined gold,
That buyeth all things, but is never sold;
It is a coin, and most men walk without it;
True love's the stamp, Jehovah's writ about it;
It rusts unused, but using makes it brighter,
'Gainst heaven high treason 'tis to make it lighter.

Music and Friendship

Richard Watson Gilder

Thrice is sweet music sweet when every word
And lovely tone by kindred hearts are heard;
So when I hear true music, heaven send,
To share that heavenly joy, one dear, dear friend!

A pet dog and cat accompany a young girl's concert in THE BROKEN STRING *by artist Charles Burton Barber (1845–1894).*
Image from Fine Art Photographic Library Ltd./Private Collection.

To an African Violet

Isla Paschal Richardson

I am unskilled in making flowers grow.
Jonquils and peonies who seem to know
Just what to do without me, I let these
Come of their own accord and when they please.
But you, exotic plant from other climes,
I wonder if you are homesick sometimes?
You now are naturalized; all you can claim
Of foreign ancestry is just your name.
Transported and transplanted, do you yearn
For native soil, or did you quickly learn
Citizenship in our United States,
Loving the friendly hand that cultivates
Your dainty blossoms? It is a surprise
That you have bloomed for me. I am not wise
In flower culture. But perhaps you know
That love, as well as skill, helps things to grow.

The learned compute that seven hundred and seven millions of millions of vibrations have penetrated the eye before it can distinguish the tints of a violet.

—Bulwer-Lytton

African violets add welcome color to a flat of greenery. Photo by Jessie Walker.

The gift of an apple is shared with a friend in this photo by Superstock.

THE HORSEBACK RIDE

Grace Greenwood

When troubled in spirit, when weary of life,
When I faint 'neath its burdens and shrink
   from its strife,
When its fruits, turned to ashes, are mocking my taste
And its fairest scene seems but a desolate waste,
Then come ye not near me, my sad heart to cheer
With friendship's soft accents or sympathy's tear.
No pity I ask, and no counsel I need;
But bring me, oh, bring me, my gallant young steed,

With his high archèd neck, and his nostril
   spread wide,
His eye full of fire, and his step full of pride!
As I spring to his back, as I seize the strong rein,
The strength to my spirit returneth again!
The bonds are all broken that fettered my mind,
And my cares borne away on the wings of the wind;
My pride lifts its head, for a season bowed down,
And the queen in my nature now puts on her crown!

The irresistible faces of two friends are captured by Superstock.

MY DOG AND I

Anne Campbell

My dog and I, on summer evenings, dream
Upon the porch, and watch the planets gleam
In the dark sky. We like, my dog and I,
The comradeship of silence. Passersby
Must envy us who are so quietly
Enjoying the pale night's serenity.

My dog and I like best a romping walk
Across the vacant fields when morning breaks.
We span each block. There is no idle talk

To spoil this hour turned magic for our sakes.
They do not know true friendship who would shun
The loyalty of this devoted one.

My dog and I have happy hours to share
In every season. There are moments rare
In joy expressed, and tranquil hours of rest,
When my dog's friendship seems the very best
Life offers, as we watch the world go by,
In fond companionship, my dog and I!

Country Custom

Harry Elmore Hurd

If you are a stranger, come to the front door—
Come to the front door as strangers do.
Come to the front door and lift the bronze knocker,
And we will open the door to you.
You will sit sedately in a Boston rocker
And talk about the weather, or whatever you wish,
While we place a birch log on the fire
And serve you apples from a willowware dish,
Fit for the taste of a Yankee squire.
But if you are an old friend, come to the back door—
Come to the back door as country folk do.
Come in without knocking, with a lusty *Hello*,
And toast your shins by the kitchen fire;
For old friends are welcome, and old friends are few.
Stay on for supper, and when you must go,
Leave, as you entered, by the unlatched door.

*You never know till you try to
reach them how accessible men
are; but you must approach
each man by the right door.*
—*Henry Ward Beecher*

The back porch of a cabin in Door County, Wisconsin, welcomes friends to sit and chat. Photo by Darryl Beers.

Devotions FROM THE Heart

Pamela Kennedy

For the Lord seeth not as man seeth; for man looketh on the outward appearance, but the Lord looketh on the heart.
1 Samuel 16:7

LOOK AGAIN

Helen was a woman everyone admired. She knew how to accomplish things. If you were in charge of something, you wanted Helen on your committee; and if she were the chairperson, she had no trouble recruiting volunteers.

She seemed to have a knack for making events successful as well as special. When she was in charge of the banquet, everyone remarked at the beautiful color scheme, the unique centerpieces, and the delightful menu. And she was attractive with a lovely, understated elegance. In short, she appeared to have it all. Her job, her family, and her home were all testimonies to her attention to detail and competence; and Helen had a smile for everyone. But Helen also had a secret that I never would have guessed. Helen was terribly lonely.

One day, when I had dashed out to the market in a pair of jeans and a sweatshirt because I was sure I could get in and out without seeing anyone I knew, I almost knocked Helen over with my shopping cart. I was studying my list while making a beeline for the cantaloupe. As I apologized, I saw something in her eyes I had never seen before—worry.

"Helen," I asked, "are you okay?" Once I said those words, I thought how ludicrous they must sound. Here was Helen in her color coordinated silk outfit with every hair in place, whereas I was dressed in mismatched clothing and looked like I was put together by a committee. But something about her expression made me pause.

"Well," she began hesitantly, "not really."

Dear Lord, forgive me for the times I judge others by their outward appearance. Help me to look with Your eyes and see into people's hearts that I may be the kind of friend You want me to be.

When her eyes filled with tears, I reached out to place my hand on her arm and said, "Hey, if you don't mind being seen with me, let's grab a cup of coffee in the bakery department." We pushed our carts to the café located in front of the bread display. As we settled at a small table with our steaming cups of coffee, she started to tell me some frightening news she had just received concerning the health of her oldest son.

I don't remember how long we sat there that morning, but I do remember it was the beginning of a difference in our relationship. For the first time I realized that Helen was a woman just like me. Despite her appearance and talents, she had doubts and fears too. Without realizing it, many women in my circle of friends had assumed that Helen was as "perfect" on the inside as she was on the outside; and because of our perceptions, and our own insecurities, we had distanced ourselves from her. We never stopped to think that she might need someone to talk to, to depend upon, to count on as a friend.

Helen and I see each other often now, and we laugh and talk about all kinds of things. She helped me learn how to arrange flowers; I taught her how to make pie crust from scratch. We've learned a lot from one another, but the most important thing is that we need to look at people's hearts, not just their appearance. I still admire the beautiful picture she presents to the world, but now I respect even more the person I've come to know as a dear and trusted friend.

Friends share thoughts and chores in this detail of MARKET TALK by artist Leo Carty. Image copyright © Arts Uniq Inc., Cookeville, Tennessee.

To Be Desired

Author Unknown

Give me the love of friends, and I
Shall not complain of cloudy sky
Or little dreams that fade and die.
Give me the clasp of one firm hand,
The lips that say, "I understand,"
And I shall walk on holy land.
For fame and fortune, burdens bring,
And winter takes the rose of spring;
But friendship is a godlike thing.

My Quest

Vera Campbell Darr

I sought for God in His out-of-doors;
His beauty I found revealed
In sunset skies and changing lights
On swaying grain in the field.

I sought God on the ocean wide;
His strength and power I found
In pounding waves and raging storm,
Majestic and profound.

I sought for God among the stars;
His light coming down to me
Revealed a light within myself
Which before I had failed to see.

I sought God in the world of men,
Yearning His love to know,
Hoping that some human heart
His love divine might show.

I sought God long and wondered oft
When my quest would end;
And then, at last, I found my God
Enthroned in the heart of a friend.

*Storm clouds gather over the eroded formations of
Badlands National Park in South Dakota.
Photo by Carr Clifton.*

Christ Church Episcopal is one of the many lovely buildings still in use in Rugby, Tennessee. Photo by Daniel E. Dempster.

RUGBY, TENNESSEE

Elizabeth Bonner Kea

I have lived in Tennessee for many years, and if asked were I familiar with my state's landmarks and attractions, I would invariably answer "yes." But as I discovered last August, I had overlooked one of Tennessee's greatest treasures. Nestled in the Cumberland Mountains, between the Clear Fork and White Oak Rivers, lies a bucolic little town called Rugby. For most native Tennesseans such as myself, rumors of Rugby's Southern charm often precede its historical significance. But Rugby has more to boast than just quaintness; it possesses a heritage and a spirit all its own.

Upon founding Rugby in 1880, British author and social reformer Thomas Hughes wrote, "Our aim and hope are to plant on these highlands a community of gentlemen and ladies; not that artificial class which goes by those grand names both in Europe and here, but a society in which the humblest members . . . will be of such strain and culture that they will be able to meet princes in the gate, without embarrassment and without self-assertion, should any such strange persons present themselves before the gate-tower of Rugby." In short, Hughes wanted to impress the world by establishing a colony that embodied all the principles of Christian idealism. Appropriately, he chose to name his colony after the institution from which he learned these principles, his alma mater, Rugby. Hughes envisioned a cooperative utopia where refined culture and agricultural life might go hand in hand, where the class systems of Europe might disappear, and where harvesting crops might be as celebrated as poetry or tennis.

Though the Rugby colony eventually reached a population of 450 and caused quite a stir across Europe and America, its idyllic existence failed to endure. Colonists favored the sophisticated leisure of tea parties and recreation rather than the serious, but necessary, work of farming. And with an outbreak of typhoid fever and the loss of financial support, most Rugby settlers opted to return to England or move to the northern United States.

Visiting Rugby, Tennessee, more than a century after its founding, I quickly recognized the alluring qualities that initially drew the colonists. Little has changed since an 1883 advertisement which described Rugby's "cool bracing, healthful mountain air; fishing and bathing in a clear river; charming walks and views; pleasant, light, airy rooms, completely furnished and excellent." All of these enticing claims still await the traveller who wishes to experience a bit of utopian life. For my part, I chose to leisurely tour several of Rugby's twenty-two original buildings: Thomas Hughes's home, Christ Church Episcopal, Harrow Road Cafe, and Rugby Printing Works. Each structure offered unique architectural design and a glimpse into early Rugbeian life, but none so enchanted me as the Thomas Hughes Library. A storehouse of seven thousand volumes donated by American and British publishers, the library was essential to Hughes's vision of a literary community. I marveled at the shelves lined with Victorian books dated no later than 1899—everything just as the original Rugbeians had known it. I could almost hear the rustling of pages and the shifting of old wooden chairs on the planked floor. Perhaps Brian Stagg, founder of the Rugby Restoration Association, captured it best when he wrote, "The most remarkable aspect of Rugby . . . is a certain indwelling of spirit. Even the visitor not generally prone to poetic sentiment should feel Rugby's spell. If he will visit the library on a breezy summer afternoon and wait for twilight's approach, he might sense, lingering in the air, the presence of a melancholy yet benevolent spirit that refuses to let go of the glory that was Rugby."

As twilight approached, concluding my day in Rugby, I *did* sense its spirit and realized that perhaps Thomas Hughes's vision for his utopia had not failed. Today, more than ever, the eighty-five residents of Rugby and the many visitors who journey to the pastoral community are embracing the founder's goal: joining cooperatively for the benefit of Rugby, celebrating the beauty of its pristine landscape, and ensuring that its heritage endures for generations to come.

THE OLD MILL AT RUGBY

Claiborne Addison Young

In Tennessee, near Rugby Town,
That place just now of wide renown,
Where Clear Fork stream its torrent pours
Past rhododendrons, rages, roars,
Then curves, then glides past rocky heights,
Now looks, then turns from grandest sights.
But suddenly it stops, it stays,
Forgetting its coquettish ways,
Forgetting its capricious will,
It stops, it stays to turn a mill.
The overhanging cliffs look down;
Their brows ne'er ruffled by a frown.
A sleeping road wades through the stream;
The noisy dam ne'er breaks its dream.
The mill stands open wide as day;
Nor locks nor bolts do bar the way.
Nor miller for his toll doth wait;
Each neighbor simply lifts the gate.
The joyous stream doth grind his grist;
He only pays the toll he lists.
A realized Arcadian dream
In this old mill on Clear Fork stream.
O Rugby, take thyself away,
Or learn to live this simple way.
Wind on, O stream, grind on, O mill
Where men pay toll from sheer good will.

*Like many early residents of Rugby, Claiborne
Addison Young enjoyed writing poetry about the
town's picturesque scenery, including the grist
mill, which is unfortunately no longer standing.*

*Photographer Gene Ahrens captured this southern mill
and stream in Rome, Georgia.*

VACATION END

Isla Paschal Richardson

The time has come when I must leave this place,
This mountaintop where I have found such calm;
There one can almost meet God face to face
Above the clouds of doubt in healing balm
Of quietude. Cool, distilled mountain air
In sacred chant sings in the tall green pines
And gently blows away each trailing care
Of yesterday. Long, misty, gray-green lines
Of other mountains melt into blue sky,
And at day's end embers of fading sun
Whisper a soft amen to prayers that I
Have breathed unvoiced. Now that my stay is done
I must take back some glimpse of inspiration
Gained on this mount of exaltation.

I KNOW A PLACE

Vera L. Eckert

There is a place where trees are tall
And sunlight drifts through valleys sweet.
Somewhere there is a cabin small
Where all my dreams could be complete.

There is a stream that gently flows
Between the hills, a lane that winds
Along the meadow my heart knows,
And often seeks, and sometimes finds.

I know a place not far away
Where stars come out, where softly wings
Are nestled safe though branches sway
To lullabies the night wind sings.

*A secluded mountain cabin in Silverton, Colorado, seems to
just avoid the waterfall above it in this photo by Dennis Frates.*

The Yellow Leaf

May Allread Baker

Today I saw a yellow leaf
Among the green ones on the tree
And felt a passing pang of grief,
Though it was beautiful to see.
For summer's days are nearly spent
And soon shall be beyond recall.
I've seen the message Time has sent—
The yellow telegram to Fall.

Summer's Ending

May Smith White

These are the sacred things that come with time:
The last rose fading by the kitchen door,
A quiet step that now has grown sublime,
The mocker's song as in all years before,
Rich days that mellow like the ripening grain,
Sparkling dew that clings to paling flowers,
A cooling breeze remembering summer rain,
Time hesitating with the holy hours.

Today the birds leave nest alone and bare,
Knowing that spring will bud and build anew.
Here lies the hope that all may come to share
In nature's plan as promises come true.
May we rejoice throughout each changing season
And know God works with perfect chart and reason.

A bench on a dock in Summer Lake, Oregon, offers a last glimpse of the passing season. Photo by Dennis Frates.

Nancy Skarmeas

CURRIER AND IVES

Somewhere in the memory of every American is a Currier and Ives print. It may be a farm scene that hung on a grandparent's living room wall, or a western prairie image remembered from the corner of the town hall, or a scene from the American Revolution recalled from a school classroom. It is not surprising how familiar these prints are; at least seven thousand engravings were produced by the firm of Currier and Ives in the second half of the nineteenth century. There are city scenes and countrysides; presidents and pioneers; firefighters and sportsmen. There are Civil War battles, steamships, and railroads. But as familiar as the prints are to the eyes of modern Americans, few of us know anything at all about Nathaniel Currier and James Merritt Ives, the two men whose wonderfully successful partnership created this uniquely American and treasured body of work. Currier and Ives were two men who turned a warm friendship and a

shared vision into a priceless archive of nineteenth-century America.

The Currier and Ives partnership was made possible by the work of a Bavarian inventor who, in the 1790s, created a printmaking process called lithography. The process was relatively simple compared to the prevailing methods of printmaking and relied on the natural ability of special grease crayons to repel water. In the simplest of terms, artists drew designs onto porous stone with these crayons, then moistened the stone with water and covered it with a greasy ink. The greasy ink was repelled by the water but adhered to the crayon design, allowing its transfer to paper. Each print was then hand-colored. Lithography came to America in the 1820s and was taken up by the firm of William S. and John Pendleton of Boston in 1824. Within five years, the Pendletons' business had expanded so that they needed an apprentice, and they hired fifteen-year-old Nathaniel Currier to fill that role.

Currier was an energetic and affable boy from nearby Roxbury, Massachusetts. He quickly fell in love with the art of lithography and, when he had outgrown the role of apprentice, moved to New York City to begin his own firm. He had learned his trade well; the firm of N. Currier flourished and grew beyond expectations. In 1852, in need of bookkeeping assistance, Currier hired a young man named James Merritt Ives.

Ives soon proved himself an asset to the firm beyond the realm of finance. He was a self-educated artist who shared his employer's ambition. He also possessed an uncanny ability to predict which prints would sell. Friendship and mutual admiration grew quickly between the two men. Within five years James Ives became a full partner in the business, thus establishing the firm Currier and Ives.

Before lithography, pictures for magazines and newspapers could only be reproduced by slow and expensive methods. There was no photography, only woodcuts and copperplate engravings. Lithography, and the firm of Currier and Ives, changed this. The partners liked to call their work "Popular Engravings for the People," and their product lived up to this billing. Using the relatively simple and inexpensive process of lithography, Currier and Ives produced prints priced as low as five cents apiece. Sold from their New York City storefront or by pushcart vendors, Currier and Ives prints brought images of news, history, and popular culture to an American society hungry for information.

Currier and Ives themselves were not the artists, but the engineers. Countless individuals carried out the work of engraving and hand-coloring, but it was the vision and business sense of Currier and Ives that drove the firm. Prints were produced as quickly as possible. If a design sold well, the stones were preserved for repeated printing; designs that did not sell had their stones reground for new designs. Business grew phenomenally. Sales expanded from the streets of New York throughout the Northeast, into the South, and eventually to the west coast. By the late 1800s, Currier and Ives had even opened an office in London to handle European sales.

The success of Currier and Ives comes down, in the end, to the match between the men and their times, between their humble ambition and the demands of the American people. America in the late nineteenth century was a tumultuous, exciting, and sometimes frightening place. Settlements were expanding westward, steam engines had revolutionized railroad and river travel, industrialization was reshaping families and communities. The Civil War had ripped the nation in two and left its scars to be healed by the next generation. America was a place where everything seemed to be changing, and in this climate, the American people were ready to embrace something positive and patriotic. They wanted nostalgia for simpler times and reaffirmation of the country's glorious heritage. They wanted to celebrate national achievements. And everything they wanted, the firm of Currier and Ives provided in the form of hand-colored lithographs at five to twenty-five cents apiece.

Nathaniel Currier retired from the business in 1880; his partner in 1895. But the firm continued, under the guidance of their sons, as long as technology was on their side. By the turn of the century, however, Currier and Ives, begun on the cutting edge of print technology, found itself falling behind the times. Photography and photoengraving had appeared, giving newspapers and weekly magazines a cheap and speedy means of documenting the events of the day. It was not long before buying lithographs from a pushcart vendor seemed terribly old-fashioned. In 1907, the firm of Currier and Ives—"The Grand Central Depot of Cheap and Popular Pictures"—shut its doors.

Serious art critics generally consider Currier and Ives prints not fine art, but popular art. Currier and Ives themselves would have been pleased with this label, for they had no grand artistic ambitions. They loved the work of lithography and loved the popular success of their prints. It is easy to imagine that they would not be disappointed today to know that they themselves are generally anonymous whereas their firm and its work remain an established part of American cultural history.

Today, Americans treasure the prints of Currier and Ives because they are nostalgic and patriotic. They offer an idealized vision of the nation at a turbulent and remarkable time. The prints are as varied in style and quality as they are in subject matter; but all are held together by a common thread. They are nineteenth-century America as nineteenth-century Americans wanted to imagine it; and as such, they are a precious and enduring part of the country's national archive.

A Painter's Holiday

Bliss Carman

We painters sometimes strangely keep
These holidays. When life runs deep
And broad and strong, it comes to make
Its own bright-colored almanack.
Impulse and incident divine
Must find their way through tone and line;
The throb of color and the dream
Of beauty, giving art its theme
From dear life's daily miracle,
Illume the artist's life as well.
A bird-note, or a turning leaf,
The first white fall of snow, a brief
Wild song from the anthology,
A smile, or a girl's kindling eye,
And there is worth enough for him
To make the page of history dim.
Who knows upon what day may come
The touch of that delirium
Which lifts plain life to the divine,
And teaches hand the magic line
No cunning rule could ever reach,
Where Soul's necessities find speech?
None knows how rapture may arrive
To be our helper, and survive
Through our essay to help in turn
All starving eager souls who yearn
Lightward discouraged and distraught.
Ah, once art's gleam of glory caught
And treasured in the heart, how then
We walk enchanted among men,
And with the elder gods confer!
So art is hope's interpreter,
And with devotion must conspire
To fan the eternal altar fire.
Wherefore you find me here today,
Not idling the good hours away,
But picturing a magic hour
With its replenishment of power.

*Artist Pierre-Auguste Renoir captured his contemporary
at work in* MONET PAINTING IN HIS GARDEN AT ARGENTEUIL.
*Image from Wadsworth Atheneum, Hartford,
Connecticut. Bequest of Anne Parrish Titzell.*

❖ ❖ ❖

A delicate hand-tinted photo forever captures a moment between friends. Photo courtesy SpotPen, Las Cruces, New Mexico.

HAND-TINTED PHOTOS

Susan Norris

For the fifteen years that I have been married, my in-laws have been steadily inundating my home with relics from my husband's past. I don't mean the occasional old toy or favorite blanket, or even a photo or two. What I mean is what appears to be a complete catalogue of his babyhood, childhood, and youth. They truly save everything and have decided that since I married their son, all of these accumulated artifacts are rightfully mine. Not only have they saved these old items, they have tagged them with the name of the child they belonged to, the date of acquisition, and any other pertinent information. Thus I have my husband's first Easter basket, complete with the date on which it was given and a list of its contents. I have the shirt from his very first little league team, the stuffed bear that his godparents gave to him on his christening day, and the little Scottish tartan cap that was passed on to him by his grandfather.

I must admit that, in the early days of marriage, when I tended to idealize my husband and his past, I cherished each one of these mementoes. But then as my home began to fill, I started to wish my in-laws had been as committed to selection as they had been to preservation. But I have learned through the years that this is a tide I cannot fight; instead, I accept what it brings graciously and then let my husband decide which relics from his past he wants to save.

I have even, in a way, come to admire my in-laws' devotion, for they have maintained this process not only for my husband, but for their three other sons. They love their boys and cherish their memories, and who am I to pass judgment on the way they express that? So, although I have not yet taken up tagging and preserving my own children's possessions (I come from a family of clutter-phobic discarders, after all), I have decided to say a thank you to my husband's parents for their devotion. This summer, in honor of their fiftieth anniversary, the family has planned a wonderful surprise party; and I have planned a gift that I hope will appeal perfectly to their sense of family history.

My in-laws have a beautiful old black-and-white photo of their four children that, although dated and captioned, sat for decades in an old photo album. I have always thought the photo was too appealing to sit thus hidden away; but they prefer to keep their photos in albums. Their family-room shelves are full of albums that are chronologically arranged, and each picture within them is carefully placed and identified. But my in-laws have never been much for framing and displaying photos. I think they feel safer with the photos in the albums; unfortunately, that means few people ever get to see them.

The particular photo that has always been my favorite shows the four children on the front porch of the family's old white farmhouse. It was taken on the Fourth of July, and an American flag flutters from the porch post. Two of the siblings are seated; my husband, the oldest of the boys, leans over the porch rail; and his youngest brother swings out over the steps, hanging onto the flag post. It is a perfect moment in time, endlessly appealing, full of the innocence of childhood, the happiness of family. I took this photo, had it copied and enlarged, and then, using a kit purchased in a craft store, hand-tinted it. Newly colored and framed, this photo will give my in-laws no choice but to hang it on the wall, safe in the knowledge that the original is back in the album in its rightful place.

I hope they will be pleased with the results of my work. The photo comes alive with its new, sub-tle colors; and the process of hand-coloring is really quite simple. It requires neither great artistic talent nor an extensive background in painting. Kits supply all the materials and detailed instructions. My kit included special pens for the coloring process; others suggest cotton swabs dipped in paint. Both are extremely forgiving. Colors can be wiped clean as long as they have not yet dried and set, and one color can be applied over another with great results. Painting faces seemed like an insurmountable challenge until I learned from the instructions that I could paint the flesh tone right over the eyes and hair and mouth and then paint the details later. The flesh tone disappears immediately underneath the blue eyes, pink mouths, and golds and browns of the children's hair.

The beauty of hand-coloring for the beginner is that photos look wonderful with just a touch of color. I have seen some examples of hand-tinted black-and-white photos that could almost pass for full-color photography. But for my photo, keeping in mind my beginner's skills, I colored only the red and blue of the flag, the colors of the children's clothing, some details of their faces and skin, and the blue of the sky. I left the remainder in its original black and white. In my eyes the result is both simple and dramatic.

I hope my gift will bring joy to my in-laws. I hope it will bring back wonderful memories of the days when their boys were young, the very days they have so perfectly preserved for future generations. I know they will wonder for a moment about why somebody would take the time and effort to "modernize" a perfectly beautiful old photograph, but I think they will understand that it is my way of saying that I understand why they are so proud of their shared past, and that I am glad that I am now a member of their family too. I want them to hang the photo on the wall, to look at it and feel satisfied at the outstanding job they have done as parents. Maybe I will inspire them to take out and display other favorite family images. And I hope, I must add, that they don't decide, in a year or two, to give the photo back to my family, tagged and dated and ready to add to our memorabilia collection—as much as I love this old photo, this is a gift for *them* to cherish.

Treasure

Georgia Axtell

There never was a day like this before.
I think I'll save and press it in a book.
I'll lay each hour out tenderly and straight.
Then, years from now, when I am low, I'll look—

I'll look again at how we walked together
And watched white goslings paddling in a stream.
I'll see again how we in summer weather
Spent these good hours and planned our lovely dream.

I'll see wild roses growing in a fence row,
And cattails at the roadside, straight and tall.
I'll listen once again to words you whisper,
While off across the fields, the gray doves call.

I've lived enough to know that lives don't ever
Turn out exactly as we wish them to.
Whatever comes henceforth, I'll ask no favor.
Life has been good. I've had this day with you.

Untouchable Wealth

Mary Ann Ott Keenan

The pages of an album
Filled with photos old
Are worth more than a fortune
In the memories that they hold.

Scrapbook

Patience Strong

This is my scrapbook. Here I keep
My treasured thoughts; come take a peep.
Come, kindred spirits, you will find
A thought to cheer your troubled mind.
These things I've cherished, odds and ends;
I share them with my dearest friends.
Come sit beside me, and we'll look
And turn the pages of this book
And dream a dream of happy things—
Of trees and stars and flowers and wings.

Life is a scrapbook, torn and old,
In which our little lives are told.
And when the twilight shadows fall,
This is the sweetest thing of all—
To turn the pages of the years,
Remembering with happy tears
The faithful love, the perfect friend.
These things we treasure to the end.

Boxes and baskets overflow with nostalgic treasures and sweet memories. Photo by Jessie Walker.

OUR HERITAGE

FROM *LIFE ON THE MISSISSIPPI*

Mark Twain

In the following excerpt from LIFE ON THE MISSISSIPPI, *a young Mark Twain has recently become a cub pilot to Horace Bixby, the captain of the* PAUL JONES, *and is attempting to learn the ever-changing ways of the river.*

At the end of what seemed like a tedious while, I had managed to pack my head full of islands, towns, bars, "points," and bends; and a curiously inanimate mass of lumber it was, too. However, inasmuch as I could shut my eyes and reel off a good long string of these names without leaving out more than ten miles of river in every fifty, I began to feel that I could take a boat down to New Orleans if I could make her skip those little gaps. But of course my complacency could hardly get start enough to lift my nose a trifle into the air, before Mr. Bixby would think of something to fetch it down again. One day he turned on me suddenly with this settler:

"What is the shape of Walnut Bend?"

He might as well have asked me my grandmother's opinion of protoplasm. I reflected respectfully, and then said I didn't know it had any particular shape. By and by he said:

"My boy, you've got to know the *shape* of the river perfectly. It is all there is left to steer by on a very dark night. Everything else is blotted out and gone. But mind you, it hasn't the same shape in the night that it has in the daytime."

"How on earth am I every going to learn it, then?"

"How do you follow a hall at home in the dark? Because you know the shape of it. You can't see it."

"Do you mean to say that I've got to know all the million trifling variations of shape in the banks of this interminable river as well as I know the shape of the front hall at home?"

"On my honor, you've got to know them *better* than any man ever did know the shapes of the halls in his own house. . . . You see, this has got to be learned; there isn't any getting around it. A clear starlight night throws such heavy shadows that, if you didn't know the shape of a shore perfectly, you would claw away from every bunch of timber because you would take the black shadow of it for a solid cape. . . . You would be fifty yards from shore all the time when you ought to be within fifty feet of it. You can't see a snag in one of those shadows, but you know exactly where it is, and the shape of the river tells you when you are coming to it. . . . You only learn the shape of the river; and you learn it with such absolute certainty that you can always steer by the shape that's in your head, and never mind the one that's before your eyes."

ABOUT THE TEXT

One of the most famous authors of the nineteenth century, Mark Twain chronicled life in America during the Victorian era. Some of Twain's most popular reminiscences recalled his childhood on the Mississippi River and his steamboat pilot days. He gathered his stories into the pages of LIFE ON THE MISSISSIPPI, *which became not only treasured American literature but also, as Twain himself recognized, a detailed record of a significant age in American history—an age when the river was the greatest highway in America and the basin of the Mississippi was called the body of the nation.*

A scene of life on the river is depicted in this 1871 print, entitled A HOME ON THE MISSISSIPPI, *by lithographers Currier and Ives.*

COLLECTOR'S CORNER

VINTAGE CLOTHING

Michelle Prater Burke

Everything about my friend Lauren hearkens back to the age of Victoria. Her home, a restored turn-of-the-century gingerbread cottage, overflows with velvet and lace pillows, and her perfume hints of heirloom roses. She often jokes that she was meant to have lived a century ago, when she could have collected calling cards and dressed in yards of lace. It's true that Lauren often seems to be a lone champion of romance and elegance in today's fast-paced world. Yet she still finds ways to surround herself and her home with all things Victorian. When I visit Lauren, however, my eyes overlook the flowered china and embroidered linens and instead are pulled toward the most interesting items that adorn her home—vintage fashions. Hanging from the doors of her chifforobe, adorning an old mannequin, and draping over pegs along a wall, her collection of antique clothing perfectly accents her charming home.

Lauren has been accumulating vintage clothing for many years, ever since an aging neighbor offered her a box of beaded dresses found in her attic. My friend began to eagerly research the style and construction of the dresses and discovered a nationwide network of vintage clothing dealers to assist her. Soon both our conversations and her home were peppered with bustles and capelets, frocks and bonnets. Some of Lauren's collectibles are treasured for their beauty and fine needlework, such as a hand-stitched christening gown or a floral whitework lingerie dress. Others are valued mostly for the glimpse they offer into past days, a time when women wore corsets even while swimming and lived with the constant danger of snagging their hoop skirts on a runaway carriage or allowing it too close to a fire.

Ever since I was introduced to the world of collectible vintage clothing, I have been amazed to see how many beautiful and interesting garments I have spotted on my own antiquing trips. I've learned that most collectors try to focus on a specific era or style of clothing, just as Lauren is drawn to pieces from the Victorian period. Yet she, like many other enthusiasts, is unable to pass up a stunning find from any era, particularly a piece that has an air of romance about it. Hanging between her turn-of-the-century gowns are a flowing crepe party dress from the 1930s and her oldest piece, a satin-trimmed gown from the 1820s that brings to mind a character from a favorite Jane Austen novel.

Many pieces of vintage clothing elicit such imagery, and the most fascinating pieces offer an intriguing story about their history as well. I've tried on a pair of petite white slippers that was worn to debutante balls by four generations of Mississippi women, and I've seen a black top hat that was the first state-side purchase of an immigrant to America and still bears the tag of its owner. Most memorable is the heartbreaking story shared by an antiques dealer who was displaying a simple ecru lace gown. His grandmother had bought the gown for her upcoming wedding to a soldier who never returned from World War I. It is this sort of history that allows vintage clothing to recapture our pasts and gives life to what at first seems like mere fabric, beads, and buttons.

On a recent visit to Lauren's home, I was delighted to see her latest purchase, a lovely turn-of-the-century hat made of beaver pelts and covered with a plethora of feathers. Lauren spoke of how nice it would have been to have lived in the days when she could wear such fine millinery daily. But on consideration, I'm glad my friend was not born a century ago. In this modern world of electronic greetings and microwaved meals, I appreciate the chance to sit in her elegant home and share a bit of her charm over tea. And as I learn more about her collection of vintage clothing, I realize how much I enjoy sharing her knowledge of a time when a table in each entry held a tray of calling cards and a new feathered hat, just waiting for the next afternoon visitor to arrive.

A STITCH IN TIME

If you would like to collect vintage clothing, the following information may be helpful.

HISTORY

• Ornate and expensive clothing has long been valued for its beauty, but only during the past thirty years have museums and collectors begun valuing vintage clothing for its historical worth.

• As early as the seventeenth century, countries such as Sweden and Russia began carefully preserving the clothing worn by royalty. In 1844, London's Victoria and Albert Museum began their collection of clothing as examples of fine artistry.

• In America in 1937, the Costume Institute was founded to study the history and care of vintage garments. The Institute joined the Metropolitan Museum of Art in 1946.

• Vintage clothing not only offers a glimpse of the fashions, lifestyles, and social morays of past days, but also of the technology available at the time as seen in the item's construction, weight, quality, and dye.

In the 1890s, women wore bathing suits such as this to the beach. The wool suit, which includes long bloomers and an attached overskirt, would have been worn with stockings and shoes as well. Photo courtesy Kristina Harris, from COLLECTOR'S GUIDE TO VINTAGE FASHIONS.

ADVICE FOR COLLECTORS

• Research to identify the eras or styles of clothing you prefer. Then learn all you can about that area of interest through library, internet, and museum research.

• Realize that the smallest amount of damage, including a tiny moth hole, stain, or rip, can greatly devalue a piece.

• After each purchase, use a notebook to document the acquisition date, seller, price, and history of the piece. Also include material that could be used to date the piece, such as a historical fashion plate or advertisement.

• If you inherit vintage pieces, ask a knowledgeable curator to examine and appraise them. You may need to pay for such professional advice.

• Locate additions to your collection at auctions, antique shops, mail-order dealers, and through ads in historical fashion periodicals.

• Look for antique ads and fashion plates to help date a particular piece of clothing. Make note of details such as fabric weight, closures, and workmanship that offer clues to a piece's history.

• Ensure that you have the proper conditions to store or display your collection.

NARROWING A COLLECTION

Because such a wide variety of vintage clothing is available, it is often effective to narrow your search to a category such as the following.

• Clothes from a specific period or style, such as 1950s party dresses.

• One type of garment, such as evening gowns.

• Children's clothes and christening gowns.

• Wedding gowns.

• Victorian "lingerie dresses," which sport shirring, lace, and detailed needlework.

• Hats, shoes, purses, and other accessories.

• Men's clothing.

The Shining Thread

Jessie Wilmore Murton

Before life's loom we weave with awkward hands
And strive each day to smooth and bring the strands
Into some semblance of the heart's design,
Whose threads, alas, tomorrow may untwine.

But there are roughnesses we cannot hide—
Rents, still unmended, though we truly tried,
Mistakes that mar the stately symmetry
Gracing the pattern of the tapestry.

Yet, through all rent and roughness, warp and woof—
Its faultless purls of golden monotone
The weaver's foil for all that fate may send—
There runs a glint of splendor, rich, aloof,
The one forever shining and alone
Unbroken thread—the memory of a friend!

Brightly colored threads combine to weave this Native American fabric from Santa Fe, New Mexico. Photo by Jean Higgins/Unicorn Stock Photos.

Questions to a Marigold

June Masters Bacher

Tell me, little marigold,
Shining bloom—a pot of gold
Arches of the rainbow hold—
Tell me, blossom, tell me, do,
Vision there against the blue,
Are you a bit of rainbow too?
What a lovely thought to send
A bit of rainbow to a friend.

Marigolds

Glenn Ward Dresbach

A jade vase in the quiet room
Had grown, with all the curtains down,
Jade stems and leaves, and wore the bloom
Of golden sunlight like a crown.

It was the time between the fall
Of grain-gold corded in the sheaf
And leaf-gold drifting to a wall—
And such a time for dreams is brief.

And so the jade vase held for me
More than the things that can be told. . .
So few dreams ever come to be
Tight buds—and then a burst of gold!

The marigold abroad her leaves doth spread,
Because the sun's and her power is the same.
—Henry Constable

These tiger swallowtail butterflies were unable to resist the tempting gold of marigolds. Photo by Gay Bumgarner.

Readers' Reflections

Your Home
Tom O. Parish
Wichita, Kansas

Your home is such a lovely one,
A joy to share when day is done.
Here love and thoughtfulness abound;
Here notes of happiness resound.
Your treasures are from here and there:
Fine old dishes and silverware,

And fairy lamps of tinted glass,
And candlesticks of richest brass.
Your cheerful fireside welcomes all
Who come within your house to call.
God bless your doors which open wide
And the lovely folk who dwell inside.

Crocheted Heart
Betty Newsom Calender
Hope, Indiana

You are intricately entwined
Around my life, as threads
In a crocheted heart,

A pleasing complex weaving
Of two intermingled lives
From a single start,

Our love a constant witness
To the endless beauty
Of our Creator's art.

Editor's Note: Readers are invited to submit unpublished, original poetry for possible publication in future issues of Ideals. Please send typed copies only; manuscripts will not be returned. Writers receive $10 for each published submission. Send material to Readers' Reflections, Ideals Publications, Inc., 535 Metroplex Drive, Suite 250, Nashville, Tennessee 37211.

To My Friend

I Have a Friend
Dean Robbins
Danville, Pennsylvania

I have a friend
To whom I'll send
These simple thoughts—
Forget-me-nots
To seal the bond
That goes beyond
What time and tide
Have men abide.

I have a friend,
And to the end
Of time and space
He has the place
Here at my side.
For he is tried
And proven true,
As friends will do.

I have a friend,
The cherished blend
Of all I see
And he in me
Casts fortune's grace
On each one's face
As we contend,
"I have a friend."

To a Friend
Helen Parham
San Francisco, California

Just a note to let you know
I am furnishing a room in my heart
Just for you.
A room filled with sunlight
At the window, sheer curtains of white,
And where all the furniture is in robin's egg blue.
Just for you.

There's a touch of pink in the afghan of blue
Where it lies neatly folded at one end of the sofa
Ready to warm and comfort you
As you rest under its covers of robin's egg blue.

The half-open window
Where sheer curtains of white gently sway
Reveals a garden and a fountain
Where nine glistening goldfish frolic and play.

This room will be always waiting for you,
Where, to your troubles, you may say "adieu."
A room where you may come and rest
For an hour or two
To reminisce, to relax, a problem solved,
Gentle laughter, all things made new.

And this, my dear friend, is the room
I have reserved in my heart.
Just for you.

My Love

My Best to You

Pledge to a New Friend

Mildred Morris Gilbert

I cannot offer fame or wealth,
A lifetime filled with happiness,
An inner peace, contentment, health,
Relief from fear or pain's distress.

Nor can I guarantee that you
Will have no sorrow while you live,
Success in everything you do;
For these are gifts not mine to give.

But I will share a cheery smile,
Extend a helping hand in need,
And make our friendship more worthwhile
With kindly words or thoughtful deed.

I promise to uphold your trust
And faith in my integrity,
Bestow, when life should seem unjust,
Encouragement and sympathy.

And even though fate might decree
That some day we be miles apart,
Always you will find in me
A warm and understanding heart.

An antique Irish Beleek china teapot completes a charming table set for special friends. Photo by Jessie Walker.

A New Friend

Margaret Skellet Spears

I attended a luncheon the other day.
The food was delicious;
So I heard the women say.
The tablecloths were linen,
The china and silver sparkling,
And the sauce for meat and dessert
The proper consistency and flavor.
I am glad I was told these things;
I did not notice.
I had the good fortune to sit
By a new-found friend,
One whose tastes are parallel
To mine: Love of good literature,
A hobby of creative writing,
And dreams of seeing her poetry in print.
We talked more than we ate.
Bread and water on a bare table
Would have been sufficient.

THROUGH MY WINDOW

Pamela Kennedy

Art by Eve DeGrie

MY BODY, MY FRIEND

When I was a little girl, I ran and played, climbed trees, and jumped off high places. I gave little thought to how far or how long or how high. Sometimes I fell, and then, as the old song says, I'd "pick myself up, dust myself off, and start all over again." I was agile, not fragile, adept, not inept, and when I got cut or scraped or broken, I mended quite nicely, thank you.

Last week I set out for my morning walk and about halfway down the hill, I fell. I didn't stumble or trip over anything, but somehow my center of gravity got ahead of the rest of me, and I had an unplanned encounter with the sidewalk. It was sort of a five-point landing in slow motion: knees, chest, elbows, chin, and nose. As I picked myself up, I gratefully noted that nothing was broken, and I only appeared to suffer some superficial scrapes and bruises. Of course my dignity took a blow, but a quick glance around revealed there were at least no witnesses in sight. After limping back home, I bathed my wounds, applied first-aid cream, and made myself a soothing cup of tea—chamomile— while I pondered the state of my body, who used to be my friend.

~ 64 ~

There was a time when my arms and legs went where I expected them to go with little complaint. It seems as though these days they're a little less compliant. When I reach for something on the top shelf or lean over to pick up something from the floor, I get sharp reminders that I can't just assume the cooperation of my limbs anymore. I recall the days when I could do a backbend in gymnastics class without a twinge. Today, just thinking about a backbend makes me reach for the aspirin!

And it's not just my muscles either. I seriously suspect I am experiencing a mutiny of the mind! I can meet someone and repeat his name twice in an ensuing conversation, make ludicrous word pictures as I learned to do in a memory course, and be at a total loss when I want to introduce my new acquaintance ten minutes later. A few days ago I was asked my telephone number and had to look it up. I made some lame excuse about never calling myself, but I think I used to be able to recite my phone number when asked. Lest I sound like I'm drawing a total mental blank, I should add I can still name all the presidents in order, due to a song I once taught my children fifteen years ago, and have excellent recall of many excruciatingly funny stories about my husband. It's just that nowadays my brain seems to be slower retrieving information of a more current nature.

And then there's the matter of my wardrobe. I used to own several pair of tailored slacks and a few figure-hugging sheath dresses. A careful inspection of my closet today reveals that most of my slacks now feature frontal pleats, and my dresses tend towards what the fashion world calls "softly flattering." The last time I went shopping for a bathing suit I was thrilled to discover a whole new line of swimwear with "tummy panels" made of scientifically advanced fabrics promising to "trim at least two inches" off me. You can bet I grabbed one of those! I like longer sweaters and looser belts these days too, and as far as I'm concerned, whoever invented control-top pantyhose deserves a Nobel Prize.

I have recently noticed that many of the women's fashion magazines are advertising cosmetic lines that are "sheer" or "non-detectable, allowing your natural beauty to shine through." I suspect my natural beauty may have dimmed just a trifle, and I'm convinced a little more coverage might be a good thing these days. I realize that little laugh lines are nothing to be ashamed of, but I don't want folks to think I've had a completely hilarious life!

This concern I have isn't limited to my exterior either. I've noticed a definite change in the way my interior body is responding these days as well. Times were when I could eat a half dozen tacos doused with "four-alarm green chili salsa" and be none the worse for it. Now, such a fiesta of gastronomy leaves me with a sleepless night or restless dreams featuring a Mariachi band. Speaking of sleep—whatever happened to those days when I fell asleep the instant my head hit the pillow and awoke feeling refreshed and revived? It seems I now average about two wake-ups a night; and when morning comes, it's always way too early for me!

I always thought of my body as my dearest friend—someone I could count on, through thick and thin (literally), someone who would never betray me or let me down. These days I wonder. It seems to me that our roles are reversing with the passing of time. Long ago, I counted on my body to help me out, be there for me when I needed an extra push, hold me up when I felt like falling down. Now perhaps I need to give my body a boost by being a better friend to it. To that end I've purchased some vitamins and a bottle of ginkgo biloba, which is supposed to sharpen my mental faculties. I found a cream at the drugstore that is guaranteed to erase "laugh lines," and I'm limiting myself to two tacos with medium sauce. But I figure a person has to draw the line somewhere. So if you see me at the beach, I'll be sporting my miracle wonder-slimmer swimsuit, and I can assure you right now that there is absolutely no way I'm ever giving up my control-top pantyhose!

Pamela Kennedy is a freelance writer of short stories, articles, essays, and children's books. Wife of a retired naval officer and mother of three children, she has made her home on both U.S. coasts and currently resides in Honolulu, Hawaii.

Friends

Madison Cawein

Down through the woods, along the way
That fords the stream; by rock and tree,
Where in the bramble-bell the bee
Swings; and through twilights green and gray
The redbird flashes suddenly,
My thoughts went wandering today.

I found the fields where, row on row,
The blackberries hang dark with fruit;
Where, nesting at the elder's root,
The partridge whistles soft and low;
The fields that billow to the foot
Of those old hills we used to know.

There lay the pond, all willow-bound,
On whose bright face, when noons were hot,
We marked the bubbles rise; some plot
To lure us in; while all around
Our heads, like fairy fancies, shot
The dragonflies without a sound.

The pond, above which evening bent
To gaze upon her gypsy face;
Wherein the twinkling night would trace
A vague, inverted firmament;
In which the green frogs tuned their bass,
And firefly sparkles came and went.

The oldtime place we often ranged,
When we were playmates, you and I;
The oldtime fields, with boyhood's sky
Still blue above them! Naught was changed:
Nothing. Alas! then, tell me why
Should we be? whom the years estranged.

Childhood memories are formed in CROSSING THE RIVER *by
artist Nikolai Petrovich Bogdanov-Bel'skii. Image from
Christie's Images.*

LATE SUMMER

May Smith White

The days lie quiet like a child asleep,
And winds no longer rustle full-grown leaves.
The farmer must not wait while summer grieves,
For ripening grain is ready now to reap.

While shadows lengthen and the sun sets deep
Within the west, the hurrying farmer weaves
And ties a band around small perfect sheaves
Of gold. For him elusive summers creep

Then pass too soon! He knows the summer sun
Has sealed her secret in the golden grain.
She worked as though her task had just begun.

For soon she knew the early autumn rain
Would come and harvesting must then be done.
Late summer always sings a glad refrain!

WHERE PEACE ABIDES

Eleanor Graham Vance

Now deep in summertime the season comes
When oats droop heavy heads, and wheat is gold.
Beyond the hills, the distant mowing drums
Announce the fragrant harvest barns will hold.
How sweet the world! And still more sweet to hear
The simple words, "The crops are good this year."

Shocks of wheat line a field near Corydon, Indiana.
Photo by Daniel Dempster.

The Fruit Cupboard

Anne Campbell

Here summer lies, imprisoned in a jar,
And autumn stands beside it in a glass.
Crab-apple jelly and pear pickles are
The fruits of autumn, while strawberries class
As summer sweetness drained ere roses pass.

There is such beauty on these shelves of mine;
The scarlet chili sauce, the pretty green
Of piccalilli, and beet relish fine
In brighter red, with pale pears set between;
And jars of jam lend contrast to the scene.

The bees store honey from the sunny bowers;
The ants prepare for snow in summer's heat.
My cupboard is a record of long hours,
But now behind glass doors the seasons meet;
And all my toil, inspired by love, is sweet.

Jelly Making

Esther Kem Thomas

I know it's almost fall—the kitchen reeks
With scent of grapes, whose silvery,
   purple cheeks
Have yielded up their succulence, and show
Their jellied wine in glasses, row on row;
Neat in their waxen caps, a tasty spread
To satisfy the appetites ahead.

There's goodness in this making jell from juice,
Like storing happiness for future use,
And in its bubbling depths my heart can see
A preparation for my family.
What if the winter winds blow sharp and chill
And call of hungry mouths is loud? I will
Get out the bread and let them spread themselves
A taste of summer from my pantry shelves.

Ideals'
Family Recipes

There are few sights to equal that of a pantry shelf stocked with jewel-like jars of canned fruits and vegetables. The following recipes (one that doesn't even require jars), will preserve your favorite summer tastes for year-round enjoyment. Before trying the recipes, please contact your local cooperative extension service office for full information regarding safe canning and preserving procedures. Mail a typed copy of your own favorite recipe along with your name, address, and phone number to Ideals Magazine, ATTN: Recipes, 535 Metroplex Drive, Suite 250, Nashville, Tennessee 37211. We will pay $10 for each recipe chosen.

Garden Cuke Salad
Cornelius Hogenbirk of Waretown, New Jersey

3 medium garden cucumbers
1 large white onion

Salt
6 tablespoons granulated sugar

1 cup white vinegar
3 cups water

Thinly slice the unpeeled cucumbers and the onion. Place in a shallow bowl in layers, sprinkling salt over each layer. Refrigerate for at least four hours, then rinse well with cool water and drain in colander.

In a small bowl, dissolve the sugar in the vinegar and water; set aside. Spoon vegetable mixture into freezer containers until each container is three-fourths full. Pour vinegar mixture over vegetables, leaving ½-inch head space at the top of each container. Label and freeze. Thaw before serving. Makes 1 quart.

Rhubarb-Raspberry Jam
Pearl Steffen of Burke, South Dakota

5 cups chopped rhubarb
4 cups granulated sugar

1 12-ounce package frozen whole raspberries
1 3-ounce package raspberry gelatin

In a large bowl, combine rhubarb, sugar, and raspberries. Refrigerate at least 5 hours.

Fill a water bath canner with water (making sure there is enough water to cover jars once they are added), and bring to a boil. Wash 3 pint-size jars and lids; then sterilize in boiling water and set aside.

Place rhubarb mixture in a large saucepan and bring to a boil. Reduce heat and simmer 10 additional minutes, stirring often. Remove from heat. Add raspberry gelatin and stir until dissolved. Pour mixture into prepared jars, leaving ½-inch head space at the top of each jar. Seal tightly with lids. Submerge jars in water bath canner. Return water to a boil, then cover. Boil 5 minutes. Use tongs to remove jars. Makes 3 pints.

Vegetable Relish
Mrs. Donald Rogers of LeRoy, Kansas

1 medium head cabbage

4 cups chopped onion

5 ripe tomatoes

10 green tomatoes

5 red bell peppers

4 green bell peppers

½ cup canning salt

6 cups granulated sugar

1 tablespoon celery seed

2 tablespoons mustard seed

1½ teaspoons turmeric

5 cups cider vinegar

1 cup water

Chop all vegetables into small pieces and combine in a large bowl. Add salt and mix well. Refrigerate overnight.

Fill water bath canner with water (making sure there is enough water to cover jars once they are added), and bring to a boil. Wash 12 pint-size canning jars and lids; then sterilize in boiling water and set aside.

Rinse vegetables well with cool water and drain in a colander. In a large stockpot, combine remaining ingredients. Add vegetables and mix well. Bring to a rolling boil, then boil 3 minutes. Spoon into prepared jars, leaving ½-inch head space at the top of each jar. Seal tightly with lids. Submerge jars in water bath canner. Return water to a boil, then cover. Boil 15 minutes. Use tongs to remove jars. Makes approximately 12 pints.

Spicy Pickled Peaches
Paige Brown of Belle Plaine, Iowa

8 pounds firm, ripe peaches

6 cups granulated sugar

4 cups cider vinegar

3 3-inch cinnamon sticks

1 tablespoon whole cloves

Peel and slice peaches; set aside. In a large saucepan, combine sugar and vinegar; bring to a boil. Place cinnamon and cloves in a loosely tied cheesecloth bag and add to vinegar mixture. Cover and simmer approximately 30 minutes.

While peaches are simmering, wash 8 pint-size canning jars and lids; then sterilize in boiling water and set aside. Fill a water bath canner with water (making sure there is enough water to cover jars once they are added), and bring to a boil.

Remove bag of spices from vinegar mixture. Bring mixture to a rolling boil. Add prepared peaches, enough for 3 to 4 pints at a time, and boil for approximately 5 minutes. Pack hot peaches into prepared jars. Cover peaches with boiling syrup, leaving ½-inch head space at the top of each jar. Seal tightly with lids. Submerge jars in water bath canner. Return water to a boil, cover, and boil 20 minutes. Use tongs to remove jars. Makes 8 pints.

Playmates

Katharine Lee Bates

Summer fervors slacken;
    Sumac torches dim;
There's bronze upon the bracken;
    September has a whim
For carmine, pearl, and amber
    Touches on her green;
Busy squirrels clamber;
    Restless birds convene.
Where Indian pipe still blanches,
    Where hoary lichen flakes
Forest trunks and branches,
    The golden foxglove makes
A mimic wood that tosses
    Warning to the trees,
Then droops upon the mosses,
    Heavy with bloom and bees.

What rumbelow of revel
    Deep in those honey-jars!
A saffron moth, with level
    And languid motion, stars
The air until he settles
    At the last pink-clover inn,
Ignoring prouder petals
    That would his favor win.
Among those wildwood vagrants
    I strolled, alone no more.
Was it the sweet-fern fragrance
    That stirred a long-sealed door
Of Time's enchanted tower?
    A little maid ran free
And for one sunny hour
    My childhood played with me.

Left: A mountain road offers a tour of autumn color in New York's Adirondack Park. Photo by Johnson's Photography.
Above: Two girls share the games of childhood. Photo by Jade Albert/FPG International.

September Morning

Deborah A. Bennett

When in these golden hours
The day dawns honey-bright
And down we stroll the misty paths
Slow ripening in the light
Of second flush, of sodden roses,
Of dewy maple leaves,
We pluck the meadow of autumn lilies
And berries from the trees.
We sit in the wonder of too-soft days,
Listening for summer's parting sighs,
And drink in the sweetness of the new-
     mown morning
And lie under whippoorwill skies.

Golden Days

Virginia Blanck Moore

These are the golden days
When over all the land
The maples flaunt the colors
Of a brightly flaming brand.

These are the golden days
When pumpkins ring the fields
Like orange balloons, and yellow corn
The harvest acre yields.

These are the golden days
When russet apples glow,
And fire flames upon the hill
Where sumac branches grow.

For autumn has a Midas touch
And spends each chilly night
Lightly flicking summer green
To turn it golden bright.

*Impatiens and maple leaves contrast the colors
of summer and fall. Photo by Darryl R. Beers.*

A SLICE OF LIFE

Edgar A. Guest

IT'S SEPTEMBER

It's September, and the orchards are afire with red and gold,
And the nights with dew are heavy, and the morning's sharp with cold;
Now the garden's at its gayest with the salvia blazing red
And the good old-fashioned asters laughing at us from their bed;
Once again in shoes and stockings are the children's little feet,
And the dog now does his snoozing on the bright side of the street.

It's September, and the cornstalks are as high as they will go,
And the red cheeks of the apples everywhere begin to show;
Now the supper's scarcely over ere the darkness settles down,
And the moon looms big and yellow at the edges of the town;
Oh, it's good to see the children, when their little prayers are said,
Duck beneath the patchwork covers when they tumble into bed.

It's September, and a calmness and a sweetness seem to fall
Over everything that's living, just as though it hears the call
Of Old Winter, trudging slowly, with his pack of ice and snow,
In the distance over yonder, and it somehow seems as though
Every tiny little blossom wants to look its very best
When the frost shall bite its petals and it drops away to rest.

It's September! It's the fullness and the ripeness of the year;
All the work of earth is finished, or the final tasks are near,
But there is no doleful wailing; every living thing that grows,
For the end that is approaching wears the finest garb it knows.
And I pray that I may proudly hold my head up high and smile
When I come to my September in the golden afterwhile.

Edgar A. Guest began his illustrious career in 1895 at the age of fourteen when his work first appeared in the Detroit Free Press. *His column was syndicated in more than three hundred newspapers, and he became known as "The Poet of the People."*

Redstone Schoolhouse in Sudbury, Massachusetts, appears ready for a class of young learners. Photo by Johnson's Photography.

SCHOOL NO. 78

Louise Cattoi

Each of us has a phase of his or her life that crowds memory. Mine is of a one-room country school in the Minnesota wilderness whose glow, despite pioneering hardships, has never dimmed. It was all so long, long ago—that golden day in late August 1915—when I alighted from the Great Northern train at the tiny flag station of Gheen in Northeastern Minnesota. I had received my teaching certificate from the Duluth Normal School, and there I was, ready to start my first assignment at School No. 78, some six miles west of Gheen.

"Take a good look at your railroad stop," advised an older teacher among the half dozen young recruits who were being discharged at various points of duty as the train puffed northward. "It will be your last look at civilization until you go home for Christmas."

Some of the young teachers were in tears. Yes indeed, country school teaching demanded stout hearts and souls that could endure loneliness and isolation. But I felt prepared as I neared Gheen, my outpost. It was named for the owner of three of the five buildings visible—the country store, the little hotel, and his dwelling. The other two buildings were another store and the one-room railroad depot.

School was to open the last Monday in August that year. I arrived four days earlier. Meeting me with one of the farm wagons drawn by a team of horses was Mrs. Sundquist, a pleasant, plumpish woman at whose farm home I was to stay. Even though she knew my name, and our relationship was to become warm and friendly, she generally addressed me by the title she called me that first day, "Teacher."

Even today, my spirits soar at the remembrance of that six-mile drive through the woods to the farmhouse. There was a tang of fall in the air. Goldenrod and wild asters sprouted along the country road. The woods were alive with birdsong, and now and then came the tap, tap, tap of a woodpecker. We finally came in sight of the school, a rectangular white and gray structure with a little porch and a small bell tower, though it had no bell. To the right, across the clearing, was the low log house I was to share with the Sundquists. Actually, it was the original "homestead shack," built by Mr. Sundquist to shelter the family while they "proved" their land.

We entered by the only door, that of the kitchen. From the kitchen a door led into a sprawling room that served as living room, dining room, and bedroom for the family. The parents slept at one side of the north wall, and the two boys, ages nine and seventeen, at the other. At the center of this wall was a small, curtained door.

"Your room, Teacher," said Mrs. Sundquist.

I parted the curtain and gulped. It was a small lean-to, built as an afterthought. It contained a bed and a small, roughly hewn wooden table large enough to hold a kerosene lamp and book. A tiny curtained area held hooks for my clothes, and there was one window on whose sill dangled the longest legged spiders I had ever seen. On gusty, winter nights I lay in bed and watched the snow seep through the lean-to's "seams."

Room and board was sixteen dollars a month. Although the room was nothing to shout about, the meals were superb, for Mrs. Sundquist was an excellent cook. My teacher's pay was sixty dollars a month. Whoever drove the team to Gheen for provisions each month would take my check along for cashing, which often meant gold coins.

Because school janitorial service would have to come out of the teacher's pay, I did the chores myself. This part of the job held no glory and required scrambling knee-deep in the snow across the clearing to the schoolhouse, building a fire, and shoveling the steps and porch. If it were icy, I had to wield the ax not only on the porch steps, but on the bench holes in the outhouse. But inside the schoolhouse a large woodstove warmed the room, and the stove's high, circular metal "jacket" with a shelf provided a wonderful place to thaw the ink and desk clock.

But the children, not the building, made School No. 78 so remarkable. The names of the students, some twenty of them, are still entwined in memory: Anny, Angie and Margaret, Gundrun and Ole, Ralph and Tressie, Frances, Peter, Steve, Burt. Some of the most beautiful children in the world, they included Johnnie with the palest face and blackest eyes and hair imaginable, and Chester with the enormous brown eyes and golden brown hair. The students' ages ranged from six to fourteen, and their ethnic heritage included Yugoslavs, Norwegians, Swedes, and Poles.

At times it was exhausting to try to conduct classes at the various grade levels (beginners, first, third, fifth, and sixth) in one room. But somehow the children did learn to spell, to read, to do sums, and to follow the Palmer Method of penmanship, which inculcated legibility if nothing else. And how those kids loved to sing! It was an outpouring of joy that wafted across the clearing, so that Mrs. Sundquist in the midst of her chores rejoiced in listening.

Fortunately, with this group, discipline had been instilled in them by their parents. There were only a few minor crises, such as the day I discovered Burt missing when I called the roll after recess.

"Burt? Where is Burt?"

"He fell in the creek."

"Quick, class dismissed. To the creek!"

We tore down the road to the creek. Thankfully, it was shallow, and the day was a beautiful warm one. All was well, and there was Burt face down on a bank, drying out.

Social life in the country was practically zero. Occasionally we would enjoy a school basket social or coffee and cake at a pupil's home. Each month came a box of books for personal reading from the Duluth Public Library.

I signed up for a second school year. During its latter half the Sundquists built a two-story house near the school, with a lovely bedroom on the second floor just for me. The final goodbyes were sad at term's end, but the strand of friendships have continued through letters over these long, long years. The ties to that little School No. 78 were never broken. All of the wonderful memories are to be forever cherished.

Country CHRONICLE

— *Lansing Christman* —

OLD HICKORY

Of all the hickory trees on the farm, I have a favorite. It stands tall and proud across the creek and far beyond the pasture near the fence that marks the boundary of our land. I sit beneath it in the early days of autumn when the sumac begins to splash its scarlet and red over the thin side hills and the brilliant crowns of maples reach like spires from roadsides and woods. From underneath the hickory, I can see the golds and maroons and browns contrasting against the familiar green of hemlock and pine.

I often close my eyes and focus on the sounds of autumn: the songs of birds calling across the pasture in the hours of late morning, first robin and sparrow, then crow and jay. As the bluebird's warble joins in from the hickory branches above, I rediscover the same sweet sound that thrilled me in April. On evening visits, the crickets chirp their tremolos, the slow-rhythmic beat a pronouncement of the certainty of the waning year.

Under the tree, there is the din-like music as I throw the hickory nuts into a pail. Very metallic-like at first, but growing more mellow and deep as the pail fills. The loud sharp sound turns into a tone of depth, a tone of fulfillment that seems so appropriate as a recessional for a fleeting year.

As I gather the nuts, I breathe in the autumn smells—the fallen leaves, the aroma of witch-hazel blooms on the pasture ledge. These are the first fragrances that suggest autumn's arrival.

Early autumn, with her clear blue skies and crisp air, her songs and scents, her reds and golds, always takes me back to my favorite hickory across the creek and beyond the pasture.

The author of three books, Lansing Christman has contributed to Ideals *for almost thirty years. Mr. Christman has also been published in several American, foreign, and braille anthologies. He lives in rural South Carolina.*

A hickory nut is surrounded with gold in this photo from Martin R. Jones/Unicorn Stock Photos.

THIS LOVELY TIME
CALLED AUTUMN

Marie A. Florian

When the goldenrod turns golden
And there's crispness in the air,
The harvest has been gathered
And the sweetcorn rows are bare,
When the garden looks quite empty
But the canning jars are full,
When the birds begin to gather
From their migratory pull,
When the daylight hours are shortened
And the blue skies turn to gray,
When the woods dress up in colors
To create a rich display,
When schoolbells call the children
With that age-old beckoning,
And another sound is common
As the raucous bluejays sing,
Then one knows that summer's over
With its balmy days now spent.
Yet the glorious days of autumn
Must be truly heaven-sent.
For there's fiery crimson bonnets
On the stately maple trees
And lemon yellow mum plants
With their frilly, deep-green leaves.
The cooler nights and crisp clear days
Are a welcome change at last,
And this lovely time called autumn
Is a season of contrast.
The great designer, artist, God,
With paintbrush held in hand,
Swept brilliant hues across the earth
To create this view so grand.

*Birch trunks contrast with the foliage in New York's
Adirondack Park. Photo by Carr Clifton.*

Readers' Forum

Snapshots from Our Ideals Readers

Above Left: Four-year-old Lisa Bradley was delighted when this little lost dog appeared on her front doorstep. Her grandmother, Dorothy Tyc of Rockfall, Connecticut, tells us that she affectionately named her new friend Taco Bell. But within a few days, the dog's owners were located, and Lisa, rather unwillingly, gave Taco Bell (whose real name is Spike) back to his family.

Below Left: When Amanda Kyne, age ten, visited her grandmother, Susan Gonsalves of Hellertown, Pennsylvania, she took her two rabbits. Ms. Gonsalves's golden retriever, Molly, found these little creatures very interesting. Amanda lives in Butler, Pennsylvania, with her parents, Sherry and Peter Kyne, and siblings, Peter and Megan.

Below Right: Maxine Destro of Cuyahoga Falls, Ohio, sent us this picture of her great grandchildren Katelynn and Hannah Rose Fleming. Having received a new liver at eight months of age, Hannah Rose is a little miracle. Ms. Destro tells us that, because of Hannah Rose's experience, their family has been reminded of how precious life is.

Left: Kelli Schutz and Victoria Berry pose to have their picture taken in front of their grandparents' muscadine vines and bluebird house in Brandon, Mississippi. Their grandmother, Peggy Nicholson, sent us this picture and tells us that she enjoys her garden, her country, her *Ideals,* and especially her grandchildren.

Thank you Dorothy Tyc, Susan Gonsalves, Maxine Destro, Peggy Nicholson, and Mrs. M. F. Campbell for sharing your family photographs with *Ideals.* We hope to hear from other readers who would like to share snapshots with the *Ideals* family. Please include a self-addressed, stamped envelope if you would like the photos returned. Keep your original photographs for safekeeping and send duplicate photos along with your name, address, and telephone number to:

Readers' Forum
Ideals Publications, Inc.
535 Metroplex Drive, Suite 250
Nashville, Tennessee 37211

Right: Mrs. M. F. Campbell of Portland, Oregon, sent us this picture of her great grandchildren, Chase Lee Campbell, seven months old, Emily Elise Campbell, two years old, and Natalie Nichole Campbell, one year old. These three cousins take time out of their play to have their picture taken in their matching outfits. Mrs. Campbell tells us that Chase, Emily, and Natalie are always ready for fun.

 Ruth F. Larsson of West Braintree, Vermont, shares this photo of her two great-grandsons, Benjamin and Bradley Thresher. The boys were enjoying the autumn color and the souvenirs that their great-grammy brought them from a recent historic country travelers' train ride.

ideals

Publisher, Patricia A. Pingry
Editor, Michelle Prater Burke
Designer, Travis Rader
Copy Editor, Elizabeth Kea
Editorial Assistant, Amy Johnson
Contributing Editors, Lansing Christman, Deana Deck, Pamela Kennedy, and Nancy Skarmeas

Acknowledgments
CIARDI, JOHN. "What Johnny Told Me," from *Fast and Slow.* Copyright © 1975 by John Ciardi. Reprinted by permission of Houghton Mifflin Company. All rights reserved. DRESBACH, GLENN WARD. "Marigolds" from *The Collected Poems of Glenn Ward Dresbach.* Used by permission of the estate of Glenn Ward Dresbach. HOLMES, MARJORIE. "Every Child Was King . . . in a Swing" from *You and I and Yesterday.* Used by permission of the author. MURTON, JESSIE WILMORE. "The Shining Thread" from *The Shining Thread.* Used by permission of Pacific Press. RICHARDSON, ISLA PASCHAL. "To an African Violet" from *Against All Time.* Used by permission of Branden Publishing. THOMAS, ESTHER KEM. "Jelly Making" from *By the Way.* Used by permission of the estate of Esther Kem Thomas. Our sincere thanks to the following authors and publishers whom we were unable to locate: May Allread Baker for "The Yellow Leaf" from *The Gift of the Year,* Bretheren Press; Anne Campbell for "The Fruit Cupboard" and "My Dog and I" from *Poems of Love and Understanding;* Louise Cattoi for "School No. 78"; Sudie Stuart Hager for "Neighbor's Garden" from *Earthbound;* Harry Elmore Hurd for "Country Custom" from *Yankee Boundaries;* Margaret Skellet Spears for "A New Friend" from *Sunshine and Shadows;* and Eleanor Graham Vance for "Where Peace Abides" from *Store in Your Heart.*